AN ESSAY
ON
TRANSCENDENTALISM

AN ESSAY
ON
TRANSCENDENTALISM
(1842)

BY

CHARLES MAYO ELLIS

A FACSIMILE REPRODUCTION
WITH AN INTRODUCTION BY
WALTER HARDING
University of Virginia

GREENWOOD PRESS, PUBLISHERS
WESTPORT, CONNECTICUT

TO

R. V. H.

&

E. D. H.

INTRODUCTION

The keynote of New England Transcendentalism is individualism. It is stressed in virtually every one of the major documents of the movement. Each Transcendentalist was to follow his own intuition wherever it led him, for it was the voice of God speaking within him. Little wonder is it then that it was never a unified movement and that it has been difficult to find a common ground on which to approach all of its highly individualistic members.

Yet there must be a central core to their beliefs or their basic premise is a faulty one. For if their intuition emanates directly from God, it must show a pattern of consistency, for to them God was the source of truth, and truth is unchanging. But the Transcendentalists themselves were not interested in tracing out that consistency. "Damn consistency," Emerson said, for he realized that any attempt within the individual to maintain a constant consistency would more-than-likely end in a devotion to trivialities. "Act singly, and what you have already done singly will justify you now . . . . For of one will, the actions will be harmonious, however unlike they seem. These varieties are lost sight of at a little distance, at a little height of thought. One tendency unites them all."

The Transcendentalists therefore were uninterested in elucidating any over-all pattern of belief. They faced each problem as it arose, content that in the long run a consistency in their actions would display itself with no explanation on their part. Therefore we will search in vain if we attempt to find in their writings any unified exposition of their beliefs. To find their attitude on religion, we must turn to Emerson's "Divinity School Address" or Parker's "On the Transient and Permanent in Christianity"; or on government, to Thoreau's "Civil Disobedience." And yet we must accept even these documents only as the beliefs of the specific individuals who wrote them and for the specific moments in their lives when they wrote them, for each vociferously reserved the right to interpret his intuition and to modify his own interpretation as he saw fit.

Such precepts can only lead to chaos, one is likely to think. And at times unquestionably their beliefs were chaotic. But, once again, they believed they had a common source of knowledge. And, in the long run, a basic pattern of consistency does shine through all their works.

In 1842, when the Transcendentalist movement was at its very height, one individual did attempt to trace out that basic pattern. And since his attempt received the blessing of the hierarchy of Transcendentalism in the pages of its organ, the *Dial*, it is strange that it has been almost completely ignored by students of the movement. In the summer of 1842, the publishing firm of Crocker & Ruggles of Boston issued an anonymous pamphlet entitled *An Essay on Transcendentalism*. Charles Lane reviewed it at length in the *Dial* for January, 1843, finding remarkably little in it to challenge and much to praise. Yet in the century since its publication, only one student of Transcendentalism (Perry Miller) has even seen fit to mention it, and he simply quotes a few sentences from it, without comment.

In justification of this neglect it is only fair to point out that the pamphlet was apparently issued in a very small edition and now has become so rare that few even know of its existence. It therefore seems wise to bring it back into print so that future students of the movement may make use of it in their studies.

I shall not attempt to evaluate the merits of the pamphlet at any length except to point out that Charles Lane found it to be "clear, instructive, poetic, warm, *religious.*" And it is, so far as I have been able to ascertain, the only attempt of a Transcendentalist (even though we cannot be certain of its authorship, I think we can unquestionably assert that the attitude expressed is that of one clearly in sympathy with the movement) to present its basic beliefs as a whole toward the major philosophical problems of life. We must however keep in mind that the Transcendentalist movement was a highly individualistic one and that therefore it would be dangerous to assume that the precepts set forth in this pamphlet would have been accepted unqualifiedly by any particular individual member of the group. Yet it also must be added that the author of this pamphlet was remarkably astute in setting forth his principles so that I think there is surprisingly little in it that any individual member of the movement would not accept. It enables us therefore to see Transcendentalism as a whole as viewed through the eyes of one of its own members. And it helps us to place the doctrines of any of the individual members, whether it be Thoreau or Emerson or one of the minor figures, into the background of the beliefs of the group as a whole.

II

There is dissappointingly little to say about the publication of the pamphlet. We know simply that it was issued by Crocker and Ruggles some time in the summer of 1842. It was registered in the copyright office for Massachusets on July 20, 1842, and was first advertised, so far as I can ascertain, in the pages of the *Boston Daily Advertiser* for September 6, 1842. Although it was mentioned among the "books received" in several of the periodicals of the time, the only review I have been able to discover was that already mentioned, in the pages of the *Dial* for January, 1843 (III, 406-411), where it was deemed sufficiently important to receive a five-page notice by Charles Lane.

The authorship of this little volume has long been discussed and has never been solved. It was published anonymously and the copyright records at the Library of Congress (It is entry no. 211 in the Massachusetts copyright records for 1842) indicate only the publishers, although it was a frequent practice then to state the authorship of anonymous publications in the copyright entry. It has at various times been attributed to at least four different men: Ralph Waldo Emerson, Henry Winsor, William Dexter Wilson, and Charles Mayo Ellis.

I think it can without question be denied that Emerson was its author. It has never been accepted into the Emerson canon. Its style, in fact, is quite unlike Emerson's. And if, as seems probable, his letter to Convers Francis of May 25, 1859, refers to this pamphlet (See Ralph L. Rusk, *The Letters of Ralph Waldo Emerson,* V, 147), he specifically denies any knowledge of the authorship of the volume. It is again in this letter to Convers Francis that I have found the attribution to Henry Winsor — but Emerson goes on to say that Winsor had specifically denied the authorship to him and had "seemed surprised at the imputation."

William Dexter Wilson's authorship of the pamphlet is not so easily disposed of. He was one of the students at Harvard Divinity School who invited Emerson to deliver his now-famous address there. For several years after his graduation he was active in Transcendentalist circles and contributed several articles to the *Dial.* In his old age when his memory was admittedly poor he told his son, William De Lancy Wilson, that "he with Geo. Ripley was responsible for several articles and tracts, and remembers one on 'Transcendentalism that he wrote, at that time." His son adds (in a letter to Bishop Frederick Dan Huntington now in *Harvard University Library Letters,* LXII, 133), "Of course he does not venture to assert that he wrote the essay in question but wishes me to say that it is very probably from his pen." But it seems more likely that he was confusing this essay with one of the several he wrote earlier for the *Dial* or some other publication, for on April 7, 1842, three months before the publication

of *An Essay on Transcendentalism,* Dr. Wilson renounced the principles of Transcendentalism and
joined the Church of England, remaining within its
fold for the rest of his long life. It seems highly
unlikely therefore that he would write a paper so
sympathetically interpreting a position which he
had just abandoned.

It seems much more likely that the pamphlet can
be assigned to Charles Mayo Ellis. While I have
been unable to find any direct evidence of his
authorship of the pamphlet, there is much circum-
stantial evidence. In the *Harvard University Library
Letters,* LXII, 133, there is a note, probably in the
handwriting of William H. Tillinghast, Assistant
Librarian at Harvard from 1887 to 1913, stating that
"Col. Higginson thinks that the work may have
been written by Charles Mayo Ellis, H. C. 1839."
Thomas Wentworth Higginson was long actively
associated with the Transcendentalists and was
usually careful in his scholarly judgments. Then too,
Lindsay Swift, in his *Brook Farm* (Macmillan, 1904,
p. 12) suggests that it was probably written by Ellis,
and again Swift was a careful scholar who knew
personally most of the Transcendentalists. And
finally, George Willis Cooke, another writer closely
associated with the Transcendentalist movement, in
his "'The Dial': An Historical and Biographical Introduction" in the *Journal of Speculative Philosophy,* XIX, *256,* states flatly, "the author of the little
book discussed being Charles M. Ellis, a Roxbury
lawyer."

Ellis was closely associated with the Transcendentalist movement. He was born in Boston on Decem-

ber 23, 1818, the son of the man who owned the
land which was later to become Brook Farm. He was
prepared for college by a Stephen M. Weld of Roxbury and entered Harvard in the Class of 1839. There
he was a classmate of Edward Everett Hale, and two
years behind those active young Transcendentalists Thoreau and Charles Stearns Wheeler. He was
at Harvard at the very time Emerson delivered his
two major addresses there — those on the "Ameri-
can Scholar" and the „Divinity School Address."
And it is obvious he caught the contagion of the
movement, for upon his graduation in 1839, he wrote
in his class book:

"I solemnly believe that there is no such thing
as the world without —, no essence of a material
entity corresponding to the outness of the pen with
which I am writing. — Indeed, the reasonings of
philosophers and sectarians about even the spiritual,
individual existence of an independent, I, — these
doctrines, though they have raised their votaries a
little from the earth (into the clouds) only force
upon me the conviction that the *me*-ness of the individual man, or mind is a nonentity.

"Yet farther, to my mind! (I beg pardon, I mean
to the portion of truth developed by my existence),
these reasonings prove that there is not even a mind,
but that truth, goodness, & beauty are the only existences, that they are interwoven in an endless maze,
that they have an indissoluble sympathy for each
other. *We* are some of their different develop-
ments — so is the creation — bound together by a
common nature; not a particle of truth can be
obliterated without destroying the harmony of the

whole. Therefore — every event, considered, not as an event in ordinary, but as the development of a truth, is important. Q. E. D." And hardly more Transcendental sentences could be found.

In 1842 he was admitted to the bar at Boston and became active in various anti-slavery activities. He was an unsuccessful candidate for Congress on the Free Soil ticket. In 1854 and 1855 he acted as junior counsel for the defense in the famous Anthony Burns case and helped to defend Theodore Parker when he was cited for contempt of court in that case. Parker in turn dedicated to him his own book *The Trial of Theodore Parker* (Boston, 1855) and presented to him a thirty-four volume set of *State Trials* "as a Token of Esteem and Gratitude for his manly Service in defending me and the Cause of Freedom of Speech against the mean and cowardly Attacks of the Kidnapper's Court in Boston *(Mass. Hist. Soc. Proceedings*, LV, 3-4). He remained a life-long friend of Parker and an active leader in his church.

Meanwhile Ellis had not forsaken his pen. In 1847, he published *The History of Roxbury Town* (Boston: S. G. Drake) and in later years he returned to pamphleteering with *Hints For Relief By A General Law To Protect And Promote Amicable Arrangements For Extension And Compromise Betwixt Debtor And Creditor* (Boston: Crosby, Nichols & Co., 1857); *The Power Of The Commander-in-Chief To Declare Martial Law, And Decree Emancipation* (Boston: A. Williams & Co., 1862) — published under the pseudonym of Libertas; *The Memorial Address On Abraham Lincoln* (St. John, N. B.: McMillan, 1865); and *Argument For Opening The Reading Room Of*

The Public Library Of The City Of Boston On Sunday Afternoons (Boston: A. Williams, 1867). He died on January 23, 1878, after a long illness, having quite un-Transcendentally "accumulated considerable property" according to his obituary in the January 25, 1878, *Boston Daily Advertiser*.

It would seem thus from his many associations with those at the heart of the Transcendentalist movement and his penchant for pamphleteering that he quite logically could have written *An Essay on Transcendentalism*. Therefore, until and unless further information is discovered to the contrary, I think it can be safely assumed that Charles Mayo Ellis was probably the author of the pamphlet.

ACKNOWLEDGEMENTS

I am indebted to the Library of Rutgers University at New Brunswick, New Jersey, and to its librarian, Mr. Donald Cameron, for permission to use their copy of *An Essay on Transcendentalism* for this facsimile reproduction. I am also indebted to Princeton University Library for permitting me to photostat from their copy several pages which were damaged in the Rutgers copy.

For various facts pertaining to the authorship of the pamphlet, I am indebted to Rev. Harold Greene Arnold of West Roxbury, Mass.; Mr. Gould P. Colman of the Cornell University Archives; Dr. Frederick R. Goff, Chief of the Rare Books Division of the Library of Congress; Mr. Clifford K. Shipton of the Harvard University Archives; Miss Elizabeth Thalman, librarian of Hobart and William Smith Colleges; Mr. Zoltan Haraszti, Keeper of Rare Books of Boston Public Library; and the staff of Alderman Library of the University of Virginia.

I am also indebted to Prof. Harry R. Warfel of the University of Florida, the editor of this series, for helpful editorial advice and encouragement.

WALTER HARDING

The University of Virginia

AN ESSAY

ON

TRANSCENDENTALISM

AN ESSAY

ON

TRANSCENDENTALISM.

BOSTON:

CROCKER AND RUGGLES.

MDCCCXLII.

BOSTON:
PRINTED BY FREEMAN AND BOLLES,
WASHINGTON STREET.

INTRODUCTION.

"Transcend: to leap over; to go beyond." DICT.

"Transcendental: supereminent; supremely excellent." DICT.

"Transcendentalism: cognition as applied to cognition a priori." KANT.

INTRODUCTION.

It seems proper, in this the first number of this short series of papers, to state briefly their object, that the reader may not be disappointed, and the writer may not be censured for not having done that which he never meant to do.

It has for some time been pretty generally admitted, at least many have made the assertion and have not yet been compelled to retract it, that there is in the midst of us, beyond the reach of flesh and sense — no part of the material world — somewhat, and what the Lord only knows, — a monster, horrendum, informe, ingens — seen only at rare intervals, by few people, in their accounts of which no two can agree, of which no one was ever able to give a description which should enable another to form any notion of the idea that was in his own mind ; — a spiritual sea-serpent, which has ventured to

the top of the ocean of soul, at which many
are terrified as much as if the Father of Lies had
in reality appeared in his old form, whose head
they must bruise; a matter of anxiety to some,
of curiosity to all.

To this, as something beyond the reach of
mortal ken, or at least, beyond what honest
men had ever before been deemed capable of
attaining to or comprehending, was given the
euphonious, significant, and, as the thing was
new, new name — TRANSCENDENTALISM. And
as the ancients on their maps only drew the
few countries they knew and set down all else
as Terra Incognita, and the people there as
barbarians; and as we, now-a-days, shade off
about the poles, unable to say whether it is
land or water, ice or fire, and enlighten the
shrewd scholar by compelling him to commit the
boundaries of the "unexplored regions" north
by the north pole, south by Greenland, &c., —
so in the spiritual world they call all beyond
the regions already known Transcendentalism.
Every new doctrine in philosophy, every new
dogma in theology, is transcendental; and so
is every plan for improving man's religious institutions, or the organization of the social system. No idea can be started for a change in
creed or catechism, in government or laws, in

the social relations of men or their individual
duties, in teaching or learning, writing or reading, criticising or creating, in art, literature, poetry or philosophy, theology or religion, but it
is termed transcendental.

If there was ever any shame attached to the
term, the censure it bore was not enough to
stop inquiry — sheer curiosity makes man go
where men do not often venture. The world
will not stop, and all ask what this is about
which so many are troubled. To give an answer to this question is the object of these papers; not to deal in any mysterious jargon; not
to make a new anglo-german rhapsody; not to
advance or support any new philosophy, or
puzzle any one with hard terms from the old;
not to propagate views which tend to under-
mine religion, overturn government or disorgan-
ize society; but to explain in common language, in the English tongue, without scientific
or philosophical terms or words that one cannot
comprehend without a dictionary, and cannot
find with one, without favor or fear, what Transcendentalism is; that if there be anything
good in it, it may be the more readily received,
if anything dangerous, the evil may be seen and
avoided.

As was said, this term is applied to many

things. It might seem to mean all things to all
men, or a different one to each. Talk to one
of anything foreign, and he will mutter something about Transcendentalism ; another thinks
the Germans are given to this rather than the
French ; a third that all Germans even, cannot
claim the name. One who has read only
Locke, says it means all ideas not innate. He
who has not read at all, brings under this cate-
gory all that forms no part of his week-day
philosophy. It seems to bear one meaning
when applied to religion ; when to style, another;
another, when to philosophy or art; in short
there is a transcendental view of everything.

   But, look a little at the matter. Man has a
body, wherein he is allied to the beasts ; reason,
which is his peculiar endowment ; a soul, which
connects him with Deity. As an animal, he
has instincts, love for food, pleasure, which we
term appetites ; as rational man, love for truth,
intuitions of the understanding, sympathies as a
member of the human family, affections of the
heart ; as a child of God, religious aspirations.
He is not merely an animal ; nor an animal
with reason. His nature is triple — animal, rational, spiritual ; and it is to those systems, on
whatever subject, which contemplate him as a
spiritual being, that we apply the term transcendental.

That belief we term Transcendentalism which maintains that man has ideas, that come not through the five senses, or the powers of reasoning ; but are either the result of direct revelation from God, his immediate inspiration, or his immanent presence in the spiritual world.

Strictly speaking, then, Transcendentalism is the recognition of this third attribute of humanity, and the inquiry must be into the history of this — the arguments that support it, its effect upon the world, on literature, philosophy, the arts, criticism, religion, and on man in his political, social and moral relations. But a glance can be given at many parts of this subject ; many must be passed by altogether. Still, there may be suggestions which will lead others to follow out inquiries which cannot be indulged in here.

The object proposed is neither to enter into a discussion of the authenticity or authority of the revealed word of God, nor to attack or defend the matters of reform in church, state or society, which are said to be projected by the transcendentalists. It may be difficult, impossible, to prove the authority of the powers that are set over us; to vindicate the forms of government or society, or the laws by which we are controlled; to prove by abstract reasoning

that *yaw* and *nein* are no better than yes and
no. It is these governments, imperfect as they
are, that secure to us comfort and protection;
these laws which are circulating the life-blood
of the community ; these forms which entwine
about men and keep them together, cultivate
the affections, make the heart warm, kindle our
holiest thoughts and waken the most delightful
associations. One in a distant land, in the
midst of strangers, will find the tear of joy starting at the sound of a single word in the language of his childhood. These things may be
caviled at by the worst — perhaps they cannot
be fairly vindicated as they are — but the best
may use them to their profit. They are no
more to be quarreled with than a mother's kiss,
a father's smile.

Every feeling and every thought seeks to
express itself in some form ; man needs excite-
ment for his feelings, suggestions for his thought,
aids to his devotion. With these we need not
meddle now ; our inquiry is in relation to Transcendentalism and its influences. We ask what
it is and how does it appear — not whether it is
consistent with the world as it is.

PRINCIPLES.

" Nulla gens tam fera, nemo omnium tam sit immanis, cujus mentem non imbuerit deorum opinio."

PRINCIPLES.

THE history of a man is not told by the account of the particles of matter of which his body is formed. He has an existence independent on the body — on the understanding — the material world or the spiritual. No logic is required to prove this. We cannot argue "I feel," or "I think, therefore I exist." The best argument to prove this is the simple statement — I am. We know that we exist. No proof of this can be adduced which is not based on the supposition of our existence.

Any theory which seeks to show that man is a mere "conformation of material particles," or " of those immaterial ideas the whole of which form the universe," leads to the conclusion that man does not exist. Matter may be in a form called human : there may be such an association of ideas as to form what might be named man, but the existence of the soul such a theory does not recognise. But besides matter and mind there is also man. If there is not there is no immortality, no life.

It cannot be that man is merely this, endowed with certain faculties — a sort of instrument; and that the soul is merely the sound of this instrument, which may make discord or harmony, as some philosophers have said. For how has this instrument conscious life? How can it hear the sounds if the sounds make up its existence? How does it feel the pulse of life beating in its bosom? Whence has it that other part which it uses as well as the body, and feels more called on to obey, which all the logic of perfect reason could not frame from all the matter in the universe? If man is but an instrument and his soul its music, why is not his soul dead when that is dumb? Why does he not cease to be when that is broken? Why does he feel within him longings, impulses, aspirations? How is it that he not only feels that he *is* — so that he may be associated with other matter, but that he himself possesses will and power — that he is not passive but active; not only is played upon, but plays, and finds within him what he has not gained from the world, what the world cannot get from him? Whence

is he? If he is but body, how has he been produced by this mysterious association? What is
he? If his body be himself, how can he use it?
If he is matter, how can he know of the existence of God? How can he contemplate that
which is not matter, the good, true, beautiful? He is not a book to be read, but he records and reads for himself.

Starting, then, with these, that man is and
God is, which is involved in the first; the inquiry is, what has man? He has body, mind,
spirit; affections, bodily, mental, *religious*; appetite, understanding, *religion*. And the latter
he has and relies on as something distinct from
the two former; not a combination of them. It is
not because reason tells him that certain things
are more for his animal comfort that he deems
them right or beautiful, but because they answer
the wants of the spiritual part of his nature.

Man knows of the existence of this spiritual
element in his being as he knows of the existence of his mind or his body. He feels conscious of possessing it, feels it to be affected by
outward objects, that some of these it loves,
some it loathes. Its existence is known as that
of the body, through the senses with which it
is endowed.

What, then, is this part of man? Describe

it. Whence, what, where? For what use? Now ask the same questions about the body. The body, you may call a structure of matter, endowed with senses by which it perceives the material world, with appetites which lead it to incorporate portions thereof with itself, and so to continue its existence. So of reason or the intellect; it is that, by whose senses, we perceive the intellectual world. This, too, has its appetites, and, making food of thought, adds to its strength and perpetuates its existence. It is the same with the religious, that which we call the highest part of our nature. This has the power of perceiving that which is independent of itself — true, good, and beautiful. For this it longs; this gives it strength and vigor. This is not doubted in every day life — all act upon it. We call him whom we find destitute of it an incomplete man, insane. Every one has the idea of God. This leads him to worship. No one can be deprived of it by education. Be where he may; do what he will, good or ill; he knows the right way. The impulses of his soul he may disregard, but he canot deny them. To call for proof of their correctness is absurd. They are axiomatic. He knows that they are. He knows that it is by their aid alone that he perceives whatever else exists.

We have laws for the body. By exact conformity to them; by giving to each its proper
food and exercise, we keep that harmony which
is health. If we break these laws we incur
pain and disease ensues. The same is true of
this other part of our nature. It may be
strengthened by use, weakened by abuse. One
part may be cultivated to an inordinate size at
the expense of the rest — and the result will be
deformity. But nothing can make that good
which is wrong, nor that evil which is right.
Nothing can deprive man of the sense of what
is right. This is the law of nature — the same
in all — the only foundation of practical religion, of government, laws, and the rule of right
between man and man.

This, then, is the doctrine of Transcendentalism — the substantive, independent existence
of the soul of man, the reality of conscience,
the religious sense, the inner light, of man's religious affections, his knowledge of right and
truth, his sense of duty, the honestem apart
from the utile — his love for beauty and holiness, his religious aspirations — with this it
starts as something not dependent on education,
custom, command, or anything beyond man
himself. These can only add new motives for
obedience to that which he feels to be of im-

perative obligation ; but they do not create and
cannot contradict the law within him. This
cannot be proved by evidence clearer than that
which each man has of himself. Habit and
education cannot eradicate it. Things may
seem painful or inexpedient, but nothing can
be just and true which this condemns.

It is plain, to any one who reflects for a moment, that these principles must bring a new
philosophy — one new in the facts with which
it starts, new in the course of inquiry, in the
end which it proposes, in matter, method and
results. All the old systems start with the assumption of the reality of man's body and the
material world, and that in the beginning man
is nothing but this body. The inquiry then is,
as to the ideas which are subsequently found in
it, of truth, justice, beauty, God, infinity, the
moral sense, his religious affections. What is
their origin ? How come they in the body ?

The question ought strictly to be stated in
another form, which shows pretty clearly the
evil of the whole system. How from the world
of matter and the body, which is only matter,
comes what we call man ? Stated in this form
it seems almost absurd ; yet this should be done,
unless we would introduce an element which
was not admitted in the beginning. Now this is

not done. From these data no progress could be made. So it is said, in the beginning the soul is a tabula rasa — a blank sheet, on which these ideas of ours are afterwards written by the outward world. But here we see the first ground is abandoned, which was, that the body is at first an empty box, and an inquiry is presented quite different from that legitimately offered and first proposed.

The true course would seem to be to ask what do we find in the body? When that is settled, the question might properly arise, how came it there? If man does indeed find within him a page written out, his first thoughts should be whether it is in a language which he can read; what it says; whether it is the same in all other men; its relations; its use; last of all, its origin. But they are not. The first problem given, nakedly stated, has always been this: Given the dead matter of the universe and the empty bodies made of it, to say how they are filled; and the answer is plain — with dead matter. Yet even this involves a new *assumption*. There must be a God, either force or Deity, to do even this. Thus this system ends in the denial of God and man.

Now this new system takes quite a different ground. In the first place, it says we have an

independent existence, for we are conscious of
it; we have reason, affections, religious sentiments, as well as bodies, whose existence is
proved to us in the same manner as that of
the bodies, through senses operated upon by
that which is without them.   Our sense of seeing is not created by the sun, though we are
not made conscious of it till we open our eyes to
the light.   So with our sense of right or beauty,
which we feel within us as soon as anything
right or beautiful is presented to the organ
which God has given us to perceive these.
And as it recognises the existence of the soul
as well as that of the body, and supposes the
senses of the soul to be nothing introduced into
the soul long after it begins to exist, but as
original endowments, not effects, but conditions
rather, of its existence, not thrown upon it by
the world, it presents quite a different field
from that of the old system.   The existence of
men's bodies and their senses, and the soul and
its senses must both be referred to one source —
God.   Both are appealed to as facts in all reasonings.

The old philosophy is sensual; that is, it af-
firms that all knowledge, the affections and religious sentiments, may be shown to have come
into the body through the senses.   The new is

spiritual. It asserts that man has something
besides the body of flesh, a spiritual body, with
senses to perceive what is true, and right and
beautiful, and a natural love for these, as the
body for its food. The question of the old, was
one which, plainly, is not one for man to answer, What is the origin of all things? How
were they created? The new seems to follow
the course of true philosophy — to classify, ar-
range and reduce to their simple elements the
objects of our contemplation, the organs we
have as men, discover the laws by which they
are regulated, and so make some useful application of them. It proposes no theory to account for their origin, does not suppose that by
some process beyond our comprehension spirit
may be resolved into matter, but contents itself
with the fact that the spirit as well as the body
is subject to certain laws — beyond which it
seeks not to go.

The results of the two systems may show
their comparative merits. The old deriving all
ideas from sensation, leads to atheism, to a religion which is but self-interest — an ethical
code which makes right synonymous with in-
dulgence of appetite, justice one with expediency, and reduces our love of what is good,
beautiful, true and divine, to habit, association

or interest. The new asserts the continual presence of God in all his works, spirit as well as matter; makes religion the natural impulse of every breast; the moral law, God's voice in every heart, independent on interest, expediency or appetite, which enables us to resist these; an universal, eternal, standard of truth, beauty, goodness, holiness, to which every man can turn and follow, if he will.

PROGRESS AND OBSTACLES.

"And Jupiter says to the carter, 'up with thee, and lay thy shoulder to the wheel. Then venture to call upon the gods to aid thee.'" ÆSOP.

PROGRESS AND OBSTACLES.

A NEW system, imperfectly developed, mis-
understood and misrepresented, with few to
support and the world to oppose it, seems always to have the least chance of success.
Everything is adverse in the world, and men
say "the presumption is against anything new."
But this has to meet more than the common
obstacles of all novelties. It is hostile to the
old systems and subversive of them. It is based
on principles which show our old philosophy to
be false and hollow; the old systems of meta-
physics incomplete and absurd; our moral code
unjust; our religion but empty show and idle
ceremony, without the principle of vitality. It
shows that the old forms of government have
no foundation in reason, and are endured only
because of man's respect for antiquity, and his
natural love for that to which he has long been

accustomed. It proposes to reform the world. Then it must of necessity be unpopular and be fiercely attacked.

In other countries, where it is older, its course was at first what it is here now. It was cried out against as subversive of government, morality and religion — as infidel and atheistical; but it spread, and is now, in its various modifications, entertained by the most religious and best governed portions of the most enlightened nations.

One reason which retards its progress is found in its very nature. The world at large seldom turn their attention to anything beyond what they can see, feel and taste; and philosophy, even, has not unfrequently been limited to an attempt to classify these and the impressions which they produce. In what are called its higher walks it has busied itself by inquiries into the origin of language or government, society or our ideas of infinity — God; or wearied the world with wrangling on questions consisting in nothing but subtle, verbal niceties, too ridiculous to be repeated. It required men cultivated in a manner of which the world could not show many examples to become zealots in such a cause as this. There have been many with bodies of proper proportion, strong and

vigorous; many of great intellects and cultivated reason; good boxers, runners, wrestlers,
fighters, geometers, logicians, metaphysicians.
But few, O how few, as earnestly bent on
cultivating the heavenly affections, as these are
on strengthening the powers of the understanding, and developing the muscles of the body.
The circumstances in which men find themselves are not favorable. To do this the principles and motives by which the world are actuated must be rejected. One must either rid
himself of the million influences about him or
spend life in contending with them. If one had
risen five hundred years ago — should one rise
now, in the midst of the Christian world, and
say I will obey the voice within, and do as it
bids, and attempt this, he would be one of the
few souls, should he succeed, that the world
remembers and reveres; for to do this he must
have a keenness of perception that is not blind-
ed by the screen that is thrown all around him,
a strong intellect to withstand the million influences, prejudices and opinions of men, an almost miraculous purity of character, if unpol-
luted by the corruptions of education and the
world, and strength of mind to renounce things
made dear by habit and use and bound to the
heart by memories of home and bonds of affec-

tion — a complete character. Few have accomplished this in busy life even imperfectly ; but their names are on every tongue, their deeds move the world. A few, it may be, poor widows, lone women, or men of toil, have done daily the duties of life, asking praise of no man ; their deeds are forgotten here — but only here. One only did this completely. He had aid from on high.

It could not be expected, then, that this would be found to make so large a figure in the world as other systems supported by schools and sects. Even now, the world owns itself too blind to comprehend it, or too depraved and prone to sin to believe it possible to live in accordance with its precepts. Still it is no new thing. It is not a dream of to-day. It has been in the world from the beginning. If men have not always seen and advocated its principles they have never denied them. All have adopted some portions of them, and more as their progress has been greater. We read in the first record of our race that sin and death came only by their violation. In the midst of the heathen world we find men who saw the light ; such was Plato, who taught this divine doctrine, though imperfectly. Christ appealed to them as facts in man, the only basis of his religion.

The facts and principles are old as the race. But it is only within a short time that they have been collected, analyzed, their phenomena observed, their relations traced, and all reduced to a philosophical system ; within a few years, that they have exercised any influence over the thinking part of the world. Perhaps, even now, their prevalence might be better proved from the tone of thought, the character of institutions, the principles by which they are sustained, their actual, practical introduction in the conduct of the world imperfect as it is, than counting the number of its advocates among the learned of the earth. It seems as if the race, as well as each man, must go through certain points in its growth. To each race in each age is given a problem. Ours solved one when they got the charter from John ; another when they got the habeas corpus act passed ; one when they came to America ; one at the revolution : so too the world in every epoch. The one now before it seems to be this : What is the true foundation of governments, and religion, and right ? The things which show this cannot be told ; each revolution and partial reform, every advance, in art, in government, social organization, or worship, is a step on the inquiry, a sign, an eddy in the rapids of the river that

is rushing to its fall. A few years ago the mas-
ters of the world said all, as they existed, were
"of divine origin; society, government, all;
popes and kings ruled by divine right;" but the
world said "no." They then said "all were
based on expediency;" but the world was not
satisfied with this answer. Now a new one is
given; "they are based on truth, man's nature,
the necessity of things as formed by God." It
is yet to be seen whether this is satisfactory.
As a child the world comes to its teachers with
its questions. Each answer suggests a new inquiry. So the world is always in one sense, in
advance of those who guide its course, and we
know less of the progress of this new doctrine,
from its actual adoption among the learned,
than from the million questions it raises on
every side — which they cannot answer. To
one who knows how many of these can be
traced to one question which has been alluded
to, and how many things of the earth there are
whose relations are determined or whose existence depends on the answer which is given to
this question — it can be no wonder that it is
avoided and delayed.

The progress of this system among us has
been not a little retarded by the character of
the Germans of the last century, its first and

chief advocates. Writing in a strange language, with a new and it may be an ill chosen set of terms, in a style fit for anything rather than philosophy, they made so abstruse a matter that it could be encountered by few who were not willing to make it the study of their life. Moreover the effect on the style and belief of some of those who had become its disciples was deemed pernicious. A harsh word or an obscure sentence was set down to the influence of German philosophy. Carlyle's unutterables and Coleridge's incomprehensibles must be all German.

In France, besides philosophers and metaphysicians, it found advocates of a popular character, men to spread abroad its leading ideas and make a practical application of them. It was no longer a matter of the study and closet, but was proclaimed from the pulpit, the forum, the senate, and displayed itself not more in attacks on English philosophy or the old sensual system than in the reforms in government and society. And here we find another reason of the opposition it meets with us. We hear much of the horrors of the French revolution, of the infidelity and atheism of France, of the danger of those principles which sever the bonds of

society.   And with these things many associate
the idea of transcendentalism.

No one doubts that there were atheists and infidels in France, or denies the horrors of the revolution.   But their cause is not traced.   The
revolution is not understood.   We have heard its
story from men who had to guard the interests
of a king and nobility, and been told that
Paine is the text writer of its doctrines.   We
might well say we had no taste for one and felt
that there was cause for terror and alarm at
the other.   Yet all this was not the work of
leagued madmen, infidels or jacobins.   The
world is not so easily moved.   All christendom
seems to have risen and subscribed the declara-
tion of freedom and equality, and joined the song
of liberty.   He is blind who does not trace the
hand of God in all.   We shall hear less of the
evils when the work is done.

But, be this good or evil, the influence of association has retarded the progress of anything
bearing the name of transcendentalism.   To
name what was thought to have caused such
evils in another country was to condemn it;
though if all the evils ascribed to its influence
in France actually happened there, it would by
no means follow that there would be danger of
their repetition here : for there was a church,

while here is religious freedom; there were
king and hereditary estate, here each man's
voice is heard and the magistrates are servants
of the people; here we have most of the things
for which they contended; and they were
gained by a struggle, less horrible, but sprung
from principles essentially the same.

Besides, the system contains in itself the elements of unpopularity. It offends the prejudices and thwarts the interests of men. The
present governments of Christendom were founded by Pagan men, and have been built up
under any influences but those of Christianity.
Of the best we can say no more than that it is
an old castle with its battlements, towers, moats
and dungeons, which men manage to live in.
Our laws have come down to us from lawless
men, pirates and plunderers, who set a price on
one's head, — and are confessedly less pure in
their principles than the code of Pagan Rome.
Our religion we have received at the hands of
men who worshiped the relics of the saints,
and burned those who taught their children the
Lord's prayer and ten commandments in the
English tongue. Not that our governments,
laws or religion are to be condemned for this.
They have been accommodated to the wants
of to-day, but there are yet many traces of

barbarian hands; men are not yet rid of the influences under which they grew. Governments
yet help the strong more than the weak; law is
not yet justice; religion has not yet parted com-
pany with superstition and intolerance. Now
this system says, the law of your being is love to
God and man — you know what is right. Do
it. And who does not see that this must be a
stumbling-block and an offence. Carried out
it might perhaps end in an Utopia. But judge
the best institutions we have by its rule, and
they will be found wanting. A child can point
out imperfections. And yet, men fight so
stoutly for things that they think work for their
interest, and look with such an eye of rever-
ence on things old and endeared to them by
habit and association, that they will not suffer
their faults even to be meddled with or assailed.

It is not to be denied that the principles of
this system, are those of reform in church,
state and society, and for this cause they are
unpopular. But the same objection might be
urged against our religion. In this point it co-
incides exactly with the precepts of Christ.
What does not conform to this law is wrong
and ought to be reformed. If the reform is
urged too fast or too far, it is not the fault of

the principles, but the zeal of those who
espouse them.

It is not to be wondered, then, that with
such obstacles, this system has advanced with
no more rapidity, but rather that it has found
any advocates. We find it working its way
everywhere ; in governments — we find nations
in their intercourse adopt rules less exclusive
and more Christian. Individual rights are more
respected and protected. Education is provi-
ded, the comforts of life secured with less par-
tiality ; cruel and sanguinary punishments are
dying out. Society shows its influence. Instead of one man born to wealth and education,
and ten thousand, his serfs, to ignorance and
beggary, the distinctions of rank are fading
away, and each is educated, and has a chance
in the scramble of life. The work must go on
till there shall be no scrambling or snatching,
but a fair and equal chance for each.

And what wonders have been wrought in
the religious condition of the race. Instead of
superstition as dark and rites as low as those of
barbarians, we have the gospel given into the
hands of every one, who is left free to read and
judge for himself. The tone of society and literature have changed. There is more that is
moral and addressed to man as man, more

that is elevating and ennobling. Reforms are every where going on to ameliorate the physical condition of men, to secure them education, religious instruction, and abolish the countless acknowledged evils of the world. These and like things show that these sentiments of right are true, and can have a practical operation. The work can never end, for men can never be so good that they may not see wherein they may be better, and they can never cease to strive while there is room for improvement.

CRITICISM.

" Taste is to sense as charity to soul,
A bias less to censure than to praise :
A quick perception of the arduous whole,
Where the dull eye some careless flaw surveys.
Every true critic from the Stagyrite
To Schlegel and to Addison — hath won
His fame by serving a reflected light,
And clearing vapor from a clouded sun."

E. L. B.

CRITICISM.

THOSE rules which regulate the original composition of works of imagination or art, or enable one to test their propriety, beauty or perfection, are the laws of criticism. It is the science which teaches us to estimate the creations of the mind, and pass judgment on the pictures which man paints of what passes within him. Its end is to enable us to estimate the worth of a poem, a picture, a book, or any work of art.

Most obviously it presupposes an intimate knowledge of the principles of human nature. What is it that perceives the beauty of a poem? On what does this depend? With what standard is it to be compared? Whence do we derive our knowledge of this standard? How are we to know when anything conforms to it? These and a thousand similar questions are not

answered with a breath. An Indian, like an
animal, might like or hate a picture merely for
its color; another more cultivated because it
caused in his mind pleasing or unpleasant associations; another because he judged it beautiful
or not. Thus there would be different systems.
One would take no note of what the others most
esteemed. So we find several systems saying
that we derive our sense of beauty from habit,
association, judgment, the study of nature.

The old were mere arbitrary, conventional
rules, founded in caprice. Works were judged
and compared with other works. The Iliad or
Æneid was the standard for a poem : the Ve-
nus de Medici a perfect form. But nothing
was said to be good or perfect in itself. Every
thing must stand or fall, not by its actual, but
by its comparative merits. Such rules had no
foundation in nature. Many of them were
irreconcilable with nature and calculated only
to trammel and embarrass. But now there is
recognised a common, universal, natural standard, which all men possess, by which all can
judge. One tries not to write like Homer or
Dante, but to produce a poem beautiful in
itself. Within himself he finds a standard higher
than anything yet produced, an idea of what
such ought to be. Thus there is one rule,

uniform, not arbitrary, but natural. Perfection
is but conformity with what all seek.

Formerly judgment was passed upon parts ;
whether they were formed according to the
most approved fashion ; thus the Chinese asked
if the feet were small, the Indian looked for
rings in the nose. Or the parts were judged in
relation to the whole. The whole was never
taken together, and the question put, whether
it was good or beautiful in itself. It was easy
to say, that this corresponded with such a model ;
that violated such a dictum of this or that author, that certain words were better suited to
describe slow motion, others quick ; that certain phrases or figures were better used in a
description intended to be sublime, others in
one pathetic, some in one ridiculous ; these and
all else in codes, of which these may serve as
examples, were easy enough. And the end
was attained. Of such materials a system was
framed. The mistake lay in calling it the art
of criticism. No doubt, it was an art to judge
according to those artificial rules. But if criticism be the art of judging of works of art or
imagination, whether they are perfect or faulty,
of pointing out their beauties or defects, there
was none of it in this method. Things most
dull, insipid and worthless, might be judged

faultless, while the things really most pre-
cious were rejected altogether.   Thus the question was, whether words, sentences, ideas, acts
or parts were arranged according to certain established precedents ; not what emotions were
excited, whether the poem kindled the fire in
our breast, the song spoke the language of our
hearts, the picture bore resemblance to our
imaginings, and represented those glad dreams
which sometimes flit through every soul — to
give a form that shall wake the remembrance of
which bright vision is the perfection of art.   It
could measure feet, scan lines, detect false
rhymes, say this exceeded the length, that had
fewer acts than the rules allowed, this history
was faulty because it agreed not with such a
model, that biography good if only a stale
parody on such another.   To gain favor with
critics, you need only conform to the literary
fashion, in bearing and dress — no matter for
the man.   One would stop you in the midst of
a song that set the soul on fire, to see — if it
corresponded with a certain canon of measure
or length ; instead of following out the train of
thought roused by a noble sentiment, stay to
remark how likely one would be to feel such
under the same circumstances in actual life.
As if one had nothing besides eyes and ears, as

if the soul were not to be roused and the spirit kindled, as well as the reason convinced, as if one could not read an oration without stopping to see how every part compared with one of Cicero's, or one who would build a beautiful edifice must go, rule in hand, and measure the Parthenon, or one would or could read Homer with the hope of being pleased with his observance of the laws of critics, and went to see how prettily the fountains played in their marble basin, and would not bathe in the living spring to renew his own life; as well might we complain, that the mighty oak, with its iron arms, and sinews strengthened by the storms of ages, or the magnolia, pride of the earth, or the evergreen pine, in whose high tops you may hear heaven whispering, were not like the trees of Attica, or the shrubs in the gardens of Rome.

Formerly men measured but did not contemplate. They read to see how one thing compared with another, not to catch the inspiration. They virtually denied the truth of our schoolroom motto, " what man has done man may do," which might read better "no man has done what man may do," and proves the truth of the poet's words, " Man praises man — commemoration mad." — All were reduced to one standard, low and mean. Limits were set to progress, forms prescribed which must be conformed to. None strove for any thing new, all was made to conform with the old. The art was not to invent but imitate, to copy not to create, to receive as standards of perfection what were but poor attempts to represent it, to look on the starting point as the goal. Thus all were blind worshipers of the past; the exertions of men were limited to trials to equal what they ought to excel. All this is to be abolished, and genius left as free to obey the voice of nature as on the first day of creation.

ART.

" High works are Sabbaths to the Soul."

ART.

AND what was art but the imitation of the outward; its end the perfect cast, the daguerrotype likeness its greatest genius, its perfection —an accurate representation or correct description.

Genius could only gather together the most perfect models or forms and copy their beauties — beyond this it could not aspire.

But the true artist does not try to make something like that which he sees; that were useless play; but to picture to others what he imagines, to represent the creatures of fancy, rouse feelings the world does not awaken. His only means for this is the instinctive common love for the beautiful, a matter independent on custom, form or fashion.

It is not true that education, habit and association are the bonds of humanity. If so, then

what is civilization but a change of the ring
from the nose to the ear, a flat head or a high
one, a coat, turban, or skin of a wild beast,
according to the fashions of men ?

There is in every one a sense by which he
judges of beauty or deformity, as well as of
right or truth. It may be uncultivated. He
may be so influenced by habit or association
that he yields to them the precedence; but it is
there, may be cultivated and appealed to by all
men; influences all, in some degree. Else how
comes it that all exclaim with wonder and ad-
mire certain productions? How is it that certain strains of music thrill through every soul?
Certain acts or sentiments seem to bring back
to every one indistinct recollections of things
that he had forgotten, and awaken happy and
holy remembrances? Why does a noble, gen-
erous, disinterested act create a sentiment of
admiration in every one, if there is not in all a
common standard, a natural love for things like
these. If imitation is the perfection of art, why
does man always have in his mind the idea of
something more beautiful than any thing he
finds in the world? Why is he not satisfied
with what he sees."

Poetry, music, the plastic arts are the offspring
of something in man better than a quick eye, a

true ear, and a cunning hand ; they speak to
and spring from a beating, feeling heart. They
are measured, not by feet or rhymes, beats, the
rules of Aristotle, or the models of Rome or
Greece, but the universal standard.

Thus the pursuits of art are ennobling. Man
is made better by them. He is cultivated, as
he never could be by other teachers. To this
sentiment alone nature addresses itself; without
this the instrument from which it wakes celestial
music were untuned or unstrung. Without this
there could be no poetry. Man could imagine
nothing beyond what he sees, utter no feeling so
high as those which nature gives. What chance
for creations of his fancy ; or better or happier
hours than nature brings. But there is a vision
beyond the sight, a language besides that of
words. Souls seem bound together by a tie
from heaven, man can quicken his fellows by
high thoughts, noble deeds, holy aspirations.

Well does Plato describe the progress, step
by step, by which from beauty in its lowest
forms, man gradually ascends, and is at last en-
abled to contemplate the beautiful in itself. To
no one, perhaps, has this yet been revealed.
Yet every true child of art has felt the inex-
pressible longing. This is the secret of his en-
thusiasm, his untiring devotion. For this he is

never satisfied with any thing that has yet been done. There is always in his mind a picture fairer than any he has yet painted.

This may serve to account for the hours of musing and the rapt moments which are spoken of as characteristic of men of true genius. Their spirits turn in from the world to contemplate something fairer. It is as if man had once been an inhabitant of the heavenly mansion, and there now and then came to him bright thoughts and happy memories, as if he "could not forget the pleasures he had known and the imperial palace whence he came."

That which is often termed art is but the clown's play ; what Goëthe calls "a mass, medley, hash, without end or meaning, where many things are crowded together in the hope that each of the dissipating crowd may find something to please him for the moment." But the true poet moves the heart by that tide of melody, which gushing from his soul, then ebbs and sucks in the world through its sympathy with those heavenly longings ; the impulses that are never controlled ; the love of truth and beauty ; "the first affections, shadowy recollections ;" the voice of nature, the truest sign of man's youth, for till this fails he cannot be said to grow old.

There was much truth in the saying, "Non merita nome di creatore, si non Iddio e il Poeta." The true province of art is not by imitation to make men think that they are contemplating a work of nature. That is trickery, jugglery. Its rule is ars celare artem. It is to produce that which shall answer men's ideas of the beauty not yet seen, and awaken feelings that have not yet been roused. Thus the true artist will not make a servile copy, nor put every wrinkle in the face, but seizing on the character, make a picture of the man ; this requires something more than skill or adroitness ; — genius, the perception of higher beauty, nobler thoughts, holier aspirations, than those commonly felt.

GOVERNMENT AND SOCIAL
ORGANIZATION.

Utopia.

GOVERNMENT AND SOCIAL ORGANIZATION.

MAN finds himself in society, bound by laws and subject to governments, with an acknowledged right to demand assistance and protection for himself, and bound to the performance of certain duties as a subject and a citizen.

The questions, What is the origin of society, laws and government? Why, or how far am I bound to respect them? Why must I regard them at all? Can they be changed, and how? Have I the right to renounce them, and when? These, and like problems, the world has, from the beginning, been trying to solve.

According to the different results of their inquiries, men have justified tyranny or anarchy. On one answer empires have been built; another has overthrown them. These answers are the basis of the economy of nations. Had these questions never been asked there would have been no revolutions.

But how ought they to be answered? By history, philosophical theories, or by reason? The first only gives a rule to make man degenerate. The second presupposes in us a knowledge of the result desired, and so infers the means of attaining it ; or, assuming certain principles, obeys them, regardless of consequences. The third can lead to nothing higher than expediency.

The principal theories in relation to the origin of governments take as their several bases for its foundation, force, contract, reason. The first, if it does not deny all obligation of right and justify the uncontrolled exercise of any power that can be gained, does something very like this, assuming that there is not any power which had not its origin in force. The second assumes that there was originally a contract to form society expressly made, or that men, by becoming members of the political body, enter into an implied one. This limits justice to the terms of the agreement. It holds men bound to that as a bargain from which they had never an opportunity of dissenting. Now a contract is a certain agreement to which the parties have beforehand mutually assented. But none such can be shown to have ever been formed between any parties. Certainly none between those held now to its performance. Moreover, it is not certain. What the contract was no one can tell. Men do not say, "thus we agreed;" but argue, "it ought to be so."

The first is the law of tyrants, the second of traders.

The third is of a different character. Man feels that he has certain wants to be supplied, certain faculties to be cultivated, affections which he cannot extinguish, rights that he cannot surrender, duties not to be neglected. Society and government it regards as means which have been devised to secure him in the possession of these. Such being their objects, they are good or bad, as they answer or defeat this end, and experience and reason must teach men for which of these they are calculated. This makes their end human happiness, and they are good or ill as they increase or lessen the sum thereof. In the words of one of its chief advocates, " Government is a contrivance of human wisdom to provide for human wants."

Such is the rational system. It is far above the others. It contains the elements of truth. As a theory, it is far beyond any thing that has yet been completely adopted in the world's practice, for never yet has there been a government or society conducted with a view to secure the greatest amount of happiness to all. But if there were such an one, its foundation would be false, taking for granted, as it must, that 'men all agree what is happiness in this world and the next, and know the best mode of securing it.

Though this is infinitely better than the others, it is imperfect. For if the justice of the first is that of the robber, and the second that of the Jew, the justice of this is mere expediency, as man can see it, nothing absolute, independent, to which he may appeal, but something unsettled, which he must reason out for himself — on which men can never agree.

Now it is absurd to suppose a period antecedent to society and government, when one strong man gained a conquest over the weak ; or men met together in a plain to make their contract ; or said, " come, let us contrive a plan that shall best secure our happiness." For man is a social being, by the nature he has from God. Independent on this fact, there are no elements of society. Men cannot live apart, alone, more than they can live without food. Without intercommunion they would cease to be men. It is the hand of God which has placed them

in society, and implanted the law in their
hearts. They did not create and cannot destroy either. In this sense government and
society are divine institutions.

Now if this be true, it overturns at once all
the old theories, and applies a brand to the
mighty piles which have been forming for ages.
Hence the bitterness with which it has been
assailed, the condemnation which has been
passed upon it without a hearing, and the imperfect and false ideas which have been entertained in regard to it. It has been spoken of
as the natural state, and men have been called
upon to consider how absurd it would be to reduce all to a state of nature, dissolve the elements of society, and allow each one to pursue
the bent of his own inclinations, obey no law
but his own will, wander like a beast over
the earth, taking without asking, at war with
all.

This is represented as the necessary result of
the principles which assert that government
and society are of divine origin, not of man's
devising, and that no human institutions can
command our obedience which violate the law
of God. But these are appeals to our fears.
They assume for facts, what is false. Man can
fall back on the universal principles of his na-

ture, and abolish laws which outrage them without bloodshed. It is not for offences against these that men wage war, but to support idle monks and priests, an extorting church, a landed estate, tyrannizing nobility, for taxes, dominion, the gains of trade, for crowns, that they fight, seeking to enrich one class at the expense of the rest. Never yet was blood shed but the quarrel arose from something of this sort. Men do not fight who really seek to obey the law God has written on their hearts.

The dissolution of society, the destruction of the present state of things, ridding man of his obligations, and reducing all to a state of nature, is not the object or the tendency of these principles. They seek to maintain the supremacy of the society and government which is natural to man and of eternal obligation. Nothing is assailed which is not wrong and unjust in itself. The state of nature they desire is not the wild liberty of beasts, but that state in which wrong and injustice shall be done to no man, in which the law of God shall not be violated, where man shall be held to the performance of those duties which his nature dictates, the practical recognition of those principles of which the world, at length, after a struggle of ages, begins to own the importance, the defence of the natural, inherent and inalienable rights, the assertion of our freedom and equality, the adoption of the precepts of conscience and christianity as the rule of life — and the end of law, the noble object which the Roman jurist proposes, " voluntas jus suum cuique tribuendi."

No doubt this would cause great revolutions, no doubt it would require a state of society far beyond any now existing in order to be fully carried out in practice. A perfect system of this character would require men perfect in their nature, circumstances which could not thwart nor defeat their plans, a sincere and uncompromising devotion to truth and justice, obedience to the impulses of Christian love; in short, it is a perfect plan for perfect beings, one that can never be realized among men as they are. But this, instead of proving that the scheme ought to be abandoned, because it is impracticable, proves quite a different thing, that it ought to be adopted so far as it is practicable ; not so far as is expedient merely, but so far as it is capable of being actually realized. Men do not relinquish the pursuit of truth because they cannot attain all knowledge ; they do not turn away from beauty because all loveliness is not theirs, and injustice is not to be upheld,

because perfect right cannot be done.   Nothing
can justify a known wrong to any man.

An objection is sometimes urged that this im-
plies a government destitute of coercion, which
is an absurdity.   That it impeaches much of the
coercion of the present governments is not to be
denied ; but it is by no means true that it denies the right of punishment or coercion.   Vin-
dictive, sanguinary, inhuman penalties are indeed
adjudged wrong.   They shock the natural sense
of us all.

But there is a system of coercion which all
acknowledge to be just ; — that any one can
be restrained who is seeking to invade another's
right ; and a natural punishment established, that,
where suffering is to be borne by some one, it is
fit that it should fall upon him who is the cause
of it rather than on another.

So far is this from tending to tear asunder
the bonds of society, that it alone makes them
certain and of perpetual obligation.   For if society or government be founded on force, it
must yield where a superior can be mustered ;
if on contract, it must be limited to the terms
of the bargain ; if on expediency, it must change
with men's views of expediency and the end of
life.   But if founded in the nature of man, and

limited by the universal principles of justice and truth, then it must be of universal and eternal obligation. Then all usurped dominion, all tyranny, wrong and injustice must have an end —but true governments, the duties of man as a citizen, can never change.

So far, then, from dissolving the community into an uncivil, unsocial, unconnected chaos of elementary principles, it cements it together by those natural, social, connected, immutable principles, which are the elements of our nature.

To this the world has been gradually advancing. Had the people, not many years ago, pretended to the privileges which they now claim as their dearest rights, it would have been said, that there was danger of disorganizing society ; and it may safely be predicted that the work will never be accomplished and never cease till every thing is abolished which violates the natural law of God.

That the accomplishment of this is a mighty task, a work for ages, is not to be denied. But it must go on if the world is not to roll back. The states which are now supported for the benefit of a small class called nobility, while the million, whose powers, as noble by nature, are, merely because of the present social system, prevented from being exercised, whose bodies are worn out with toil, whose intellects are left dead, and the holy affections of the heart smothered as if they would blaze forth with a light that might lead them out of the vale of misery and shame, are doomed to toil and death, — these states must fall, for they are founded on wrong and injustice.

And so must, and so ought to fall many social institutions, maxims on which men act in their intercourse with each other, rules of law, which claiming to be framed for securing justice between man and man, actually help them to deal unjustly by each other, and principles on which they pretend to act as religious beings. For instance, the laws for the distribution of property and the provision for education in most of the countries of Europe, where one is born in the lap of wealth, and merely from the frame of society, sustained there at the expense of a thousand who, from the same cause, are doomed to worse than death ; the rules of trade, which allow one man to take any advantage of another not amounting to positive fraud ; the Christian love seen in British manufactories, where five hundred children work under the lash for seventeen hours a day, while their parents starve, and their employers (not owners, for there all

are free,) waste in riotous living the gold that
is washed from the sands of life by the blood
of innocent hearts. These things, and many
that could be named, must fall, if it be true that
there is in man a sense of what is just and
true.

Must existing institutions be destroyed, certain classes of society be ruined, trades, hitherto honorable, be abolished, and all be changed?
The answer is plain. What is wrong ought not
to be. The misery to fall on a few is nothing
to that daily endured by many now — is the
meet wages of wrong, and is not to be weighed
against the common happiness.

But the changes required are far less than
one might imagine, or the naked statement lead
one to suppose. Few things spring from actual
evil, but from a perversion of good, an adherence to things after their uses have ended, from
interest or habit. Men, individually, are good
at heart, and, collectively, act rather from false
reasoning and mistaken principles than base and
unworthy motives. It is only a few forms that
require change. The chief obstacle to be over-
come is prejudice. The only danger to be
feared, that doctrines shall be extended beyond
their legitimate sphere. The best means to
further the work, the education, physical, men-

tal, moral, of all men. Bloody revolutions are not requisite, nor charters, petitions, nor declarations. Fast as man grows better the holy work goes on. Things accommodate themselves to his wants, silently, but continually. When the only objection urged is, that man is not good enough to receive it, one need not search long to find where lies the fault.

RELIGION.

"From this foolish mixture of divine and human things,
there results not only a fantastic philosophy, but a heretical
religion."   BAC.

Squire. "Well, Deacon, how did you like the sermon to-
day?"

Deacon. "Why, I thought it was pretty transcendental,
ha?"

Squire. "Yes, yes, very good indeed; spiritual, what all
should live."

Deacon. "Very bad, indeed. Infidel. Dangerous."

Squire's wife. "La, I could not comprehend a word of it."

Deacon's daughter. "Why it all seemed as plain as light
to me. Every one would believe it if it were not so true."

The GOSSIP.

RELIGION.

But it is from the influence of the Transcendental philosophy on religion that the most
important results are anticipated.   And, as this
is a subject of much interest and moment, let us
consider what is the true question at issue —
that it may have the merit that belongs to it
and no more, and may be condemned for no
more heresies than it introduces.

Transcendentalism is predicated on the reality
of the spiritual or religious element in man ; his
inborn capacity to perceive truth and right, so
that moral and religious truths can be proved to
him with the same degree of certainty that at-
tends mathematical demonstration ; and for the
same reason, because they can be shown to
conform to certain fundamental truths, axioms,
which all know, none can prove or deny, beyond which we cannot go.   It presents no

question as to the divine origin of the Sabbath
or church; none in relation to the authenticity
or authority of the old or new testament, their
infallible or plenary inspiration. These are for
critics, historians, divines, theologians. It has
nothing to do with the trinity or unity, the humanity or divinity of the Saviour. In short, it
relates to nothing that is in any wise connected
with biblical criticism or theology. These are
matters intimately connected with and often
taken for religion itself; but they are distinct
from it, and the most religious man may be en-
tirely ignorant of them. He who can hear the
word, believe and obey, is religious.

The true inquiry is a question of fact, on
which few in their better moments of reflec-
tion would hesitate to answer, but which the
world practically denies. Now the proofs which
Transcendentalism adduces to show the reality
of truth, goodness, beauty and man's natural
reliance on a superior being — God, and his
innate sense of right and justice, may be sum-
med up briefly as follows:

1. Experience. We have found it in ourselves, and regulated our conduct accordingly.
We feel ourselves impelled to obey this natural
love as much as the appetite for food. We
feel pain when its wants are not satisfied or its

sense violated, as well as from the breach of any other law of our nature. We know that we have this, as we know that we have bodies. We are conscious of having and using them. Through them we derive certain sensations, and gain knowledge of what is not part of ourselves.

2. All men recognise its existence; act upon it when they are not induced to do otherwise; and then they are conscious of a violation of the law of their nature. All speak of things as good, right, or beautiful in themselves, independently of interest or association. All appeal to the common sense of men. This standard is not varied by education or civilization, but is the same every where and always.

3. If one is deprived of this he ceases to be a man. The moral sense, the power to distinguish between right and wrong, is the attribute of man.

Without this there could be no sin. If man were but a bundle of sensations, there could be nothing to control the animal impulses, the dictates of appetite; there would be no moral freedom or accountability. Without moral sense there could be no moral offence.

The Saviour appealed to this as the foundation of all religion; our innate sense of right and goodness. For this reason he called reli-

gion a thing so simple a child can comprehend
it all. Obedience to this he made the substance of religion.

It does exist, then. And clearly it is the
only life of religion. All that is founded on
any thing else is false. Any moral argument
addressed to aught else than the sense of right,
which Christ appealed to; any worship which
is not warmed by that natural love implanted
in each man by his Creator, is not religion.
And here there would be no difference between
men; they would not quarrel when told they
must do what is right and obey conscience;
were it not for the strange anomaly, most of
the institutions of the world called Christian
are based on a philosophy which logically denies the truth of all religion. Men seek to live
without that, without which Christ said no man
can live.

Christianity cannot exist with sensualism,
materialism. They deny the existence of those
heaven-born affections and holy aspirations on
which it alone relies. These refer all through
the mind to the body, but that is the religion of
the heart. Christianity is spiritualism applied
to life; the cultivation of the divine part of
man; the pursuit of goodness, truth, beauty,
obedience to right, adherence to duty, not from

pleasure, interest present or future, or habit or
fear, but because it is the call of nature, which
must be obeyed, for which no reason can be
given stronger than that it is right, and God has
made it pleasing in our sight.

It may be asked, then, if religion was dead
for centuries before the rise of this spiritual philosophy. The reply is not easily made. So
far as this has been denied, christianity has
been rejected. And of those by whom the
world is commonly judged, this statement, sad
as it seems, is true. They seem to have denied
their master. Else forms could not have been
deemed so vital, creeds so necessary, popes and
priests could not have pardoned, bishops could
not have excommunicated, men would not have
been burned or stoned for teaching their children the Lord's prayer in the English tongue,
nor been denounced as atheist or infidel for saying that they believed and worshipped, not on
the authority of priests or councils, not from
fear or interest, but because the truths of religion they knew and felt, and they could not
stop the pulse that beats in every soul.

Those called the church, perhaps, have never
fully adopted the popular philosophy. In its
extent it could not be reconciled with religion.
One was of earth, the other of heaven. Yet

even they have drunk enough of the poisoned pool to cause sickness and death. The evils in the church with which the reformers waged war, sprung from the sensual philosophy, and the greatest errors found in the religious systems of this day are those which have been born of the same earthy, sordid, bestial ideas.

If it had not been that the religious element in man is a spring that is never dry, christianity might now exist only as the ghost of the church. But let philosophers argue as they will, and prove that there is no right, no God ; let governments and society be organized as they may ; let divines appeal to our interest instead of our conscience, and sacrifice religion and reason on the altar of flesh and sense, — the great mass of mankind are still governed by the principles of common sense, the inherent knowledge of truth, the natural love of right, the instinctive sense and love of God. Their minds and hearts are their own. They feel within them a power to withstand the influence of things that are false.

These facts may serve to account for the common remark that there are more skeptics within the church than without it, and that men have been made infidels by the arguments of christian disciples. They are skeptics only in relation to the philosophy and morality advocated by men calling themselves christians. They disbelieve the arguments by which christianity is sustained, because they are convinced of the reality of actual religion. They know the truth of their religious nature. Revealed religion is doubted only when men seek to make it something hostile to natural religion; whereas it is only its supplement. And herein they are right. It is more likely that men should be false, and records erroneous, than that God should contradict himself.

There is some truth in the saying that it is among the educated men that disbelief is found. Not that ignorance is better for man, or all he can know is "nothing can be known." It is not knowledge, but belief and study of falsehood that has been his bane. In truth, those for centuries, who were learned at all, have been imbued with principles which strike at the root of all faith; and are not to be reconciled with religion, natural or revealed. Their worship was but superstition.

Hence arose a large class who adopted natural religion; men who perceived the errors of the former class, but took no pains to ask their origin. They rejected the mummery of juggling priests and their relics; and seeing that

what they called the revealed word could not
be sustained, save by the sacrifice of human
nature, they renounced it without inquiry.
Those only, who, having made religion a study,
have been so free from the prejudices of early
education, the principles of the popular philosophy, the influences of the old theology, that
they could look at the revealed word with the
eye of reason and call conscience and the heart
to their aid in its interpretation, they alone have
been the true believers, though seldom counted
such, and but few in number.

Now the aim of the spiritual philosophy is to
make all men inquirers and true believers. It is
no system which may lead men astray. It rests
on no arguments which can lead one to question the truth of religion. It forms no creeds,
adopts no rules of faith or practice, organizes
no body which shall compel men to receive or
reject it. The results to which it leads are
identical with those of revelation. It cannot
endanger religion, for it is religion. The reality of right and truth, the supremacy of conscience, the eternal obligation of duty, independent on interest, pleasure, or spiritual cen-
sures; these belong equally to this and to
christianity. The completeness of our being,
which is the doctrine of one, and the perfect

life, which the other enjoins, are the same. The end of each is the beauty of holiness.

But it is said that these principles lead to doctrines concerning the Saviour, and rules of interpreting the scriptures which utterly destroy the christian religion as a divine revelation; or, at least, lead to views in relation to it which are adapted only to a few pure and cultivated, but which would have no more control over the mass than absolute atheism; for they need some form and must be bound by some rites and observances. Take, as examples, the humanity of the Saviour, and the rational interpretation of the scriptures.

The humanity of Christ is no new doctrine, having been held by his immediate followers. It sounds more harshly when stated in this form than another, the divinity of man. No one can doubt that he spoke of man as endowed with an infallible guide in all that relates to his duty. He spoke of him as created in the image of God: he commanded him to be perfect.

Let any one consider for a moment, and he will own that it is only because of circumstances, because man does not obey and cultivate the affections of his heart, that he does not live a perfect blameless life, and not from any incapacity in the nature he is endowed with. If he is incapable of perfection, what is the limit to his attainments? Why is no one so good that he can be no better? Why is there always before each an idea of something higher than what he has yet gained? That it is the duty of man to live in accordance with the dictates of the inner sense, and that it is a correct guide given us by God, can hardly be denied by a Christian.

Still, it is said, if it was only this human nature that he possessed, if he was the son of God in no peculiar sense, if he differed from us only in being infinitely better, was endowed with no power which we may not gain, spoke from no special inspiration, there is an end of christianity; man is thrown upon himself again, and may pass judgment on the bible without being bound to obey its commands. These conclusions so violate all that we believe, and desecrate what we have always reverenced, that few will fairly examine, and most reject at once any system from which they are said to result. But the true course of inquiry is not whether the conclusions are unsatisfactory, but whether the premises are true, and they are legitimately deduced from them.

Let us then start with these assertions, God made man in his own image; Be perfect as

your Father in heaven, and the like, and take
them in their natural sense, and see if they lead
to conclusions so absurd as to show that we
must have been in error.

Now the argument is this; beings having the
same natures, have the same powers. If our
natures are the same with that of Christ, our
powers are the same. Upon the different parts
of this, the world has always been divided; and
thousands have laid down life in defence of one
or the other of these propositions.

The fallacy seems to be in the word same.
In the first proposition it is used generally as
implying identity or likeness in all particulars;
in the next, it must be received in a limited
sense, — of like kind and attributes, not the
same in degree. But perhaps this difference in
the degree of development will account for all.
Every one who reveals to us a new truth, speaks
with the voice of authority : we bow before one
who points out our faults, and is better than we
are ; we acknowledge the inspiration of one
who advocates what is right and true ; we feel
our own when we loathe and detest what is
base and impure. What shall we say, then, of
one who was infinitely our superior ? whom
God saw fit to make perfect, that man might
see of what he was capable ? There is no log-

ical inconsistency in acknowleding the authority
and superior power of one who had a nature
similar to our own. But there is an absurdity in calling on us to imitate one of a different
nature.

It is urged that this annihilates the argument
from the evidence of miracles. But, assuming
that Christianity rests upon the authority of
miracles, it has not been shown that the power
of working them is not the result of human perfection. We count nothing miraculous that is
done by common men. But were we all in a
state of ignorance, and should one come among
us, such as we now consider a mere common
man, the wonders he would work merely from
his knowledge of astronomy, the sciences, arts,
mechanics, would seem to us only to be ascribed to miraculous power. And if to this be
added the character of a teacher of the present
religious principles, we should do homage to
him as a divinity. Such, we know, has been
the course of the world hitherto. Now Christ
had all the knowledge that man can possess.
Consequently, his works must always, to all
men, so long as they remain imperfect, appear miraculous; though in themselves they
were no violations of God's laws, but the result
of his knowledge and perfect observance of those
laws.

This is the only view which gives to his life any significance. If it were the result of different powers, it can be no example to us. He can be no pattern to regulate the conduct of moral beings who was incapable of sin. If he was not human, then was there no merit in that which most claims our admiration; and the life, which we are accustomed to regard as a holy copy for our imitation, was but a deception. He was never tempted, never prayed, never suffered, bore no cross; his resurrection is no proof of our immortality. If, on the other hand, his nature was like ours, all is plain, and there is no room for doubt or distrust. This idea of his humanity does not deny the special interposition of God in miracles, and does not deny the divine authority of the Saviour. It attributes to every one the like kind of inspiration, though incomplete. There is in each the power of seeing the truth; all actual love for it, which, as it is in us, is common sense, conscience, the moral sense, the religious, spiritual part of our nature, to which in its completeness we give the name inspiration.

In speaking of all men, then, as in a certain sense inspired, we do not say that they are on an equality with the Saviour, or that he has no authority over them. But only this; that it is because they are inspired that they can understand him. You cannot talk of colors to a blind man, or reason with one who is insane; nor can you speak of truth, beauty, virtue, or appeal to one as a religious being, who has no inspiration.

The dangers of this doctrine seem altogether imaginary. It can lead no one to question the truth of religion; at most only inducing a new ground of belief. It makes religion more a matter of the heart than the head, of motives than works, of feeling than reasoning, of duty than interest, of faith than of evidence.

Practically, its tendencies are infinitely nobler and higher. Teaching that man has the inborn knowledge of what is right, true and beautiful, a natural love for them; its motto is duty, its path rectitude, its aim perfection. It never suffers man to be content with what he is, saying always that he may be better than he is, bidding him to do his duty and trust in his God. No evil can come of this.

The only objection is, that this seeks to introduce a standard too high, a morality too exact, a philosophy too spiritual, a religion too exalted for the world as it is. Alas! for the reason, the world is too bad to be made better; too dead to be raised; too sinful to be saved. But it is not so. The objection is specious. The world cannot receive this system as it is ; it will grow better by receiving it. There is no danger, no mystery to man. The trouble is to do the work. If there is danger in calling on men to be better, from better motives, it is to things not founded in truth.

2. The rational interpretation. — Many confound Transcendentalism with what may be denoted rationalism. The former owns the authority of revelation because of our intuitive perception of its truth. The latter says, that the Bible is to be taken like any other book, written by and for reasonable beings, and to be rejected or received according as it approves itself to our understanding. The distinction is obvious.

That the sacred writings are to receive a rational interpretation none would deny ; but few would admit that we are to exercise the same rational interpretation in relation to this which we apply to other works. All feel that this is no common book. None view it as they would another. It is an inspired book. To some, completely, infallibly so ; so that to doubt a word is as bad as to deny the whole ; accounts must be believed, though science and history show they are not correct ; nay, state-

ments directly conflicting with each other must
be received.   Others only regard the New Testament as infallible in religious matters, and receive the Old only as the most ancient of histo-
ries, inestimable as a narrative of the olden times,
and illustrative of the New, but of no intrinsic
authority.   But they will not attempt to account for the contradictions and inconsistencies
in this.   They either say they will not question ; they take things as they are ; there are
figurative expressions ; differences on minor
points, proofs, rather, of the authenticity of the
whole ; perhaps, interpolations.   One class only
is consistent in its action, those who maintain the
plenary and infallible inspiration of the whole,
and all connected with it.   But this is catholi-
cism, most bigoted.   Once leave this, and we
cannot stop till we apply to this the rules of
construction, which address themselves to the
common understanding.   It can never be understood and vindicated, till tested by the universal principles of evidence.   It cannot be
read as one work.   The inquiries are to be made
of each book, When was it written ; where ; by
whom ; for what end ; what does it purport to
be.   An answer to these questions would quiet
many.   To these questions different answers
must be given.   All, then, cannot be the word

of God, written for all times and all men. If
the whole is presented to one as the infallible
word of God, the whole must be rejected. But
all can be reconciled. All is clear enough if
we say that each book is to be received and
read according to what it pretends to be, and
the circumstances under which it was written.
Present the book to any one in this light, and
he can have no ground to say it is false. But
say, it is more than this, and you give reason for
the rejection of all, by claiming more than you
can maintain. This is the only view in which
the scriptures can safely be presented to any
one. This is the only view in which apparent
inconsistencies will not lead to disbelief. But
under this we should be led to expect to find
them, and should thereby be led to question
the authenticity of the whole no more than we
should doubt the early history of New England
because Cotton Mather and the rest believed
in witchcraft, or doubt there was such a per-
son as Washington, because historians differ in
some circumstances and views of his character.
Let the Bible be presented to ten men of ma-
ture minds, cultivated and learned, but who had
never examined it, as the infallible word of
God, to claim their implicit belief, and they
would not finish the first chapter before they

would say, " It cannot be." But give it to
them as a record containing the lives of the
best men, the thoughts of inspired ones, the devotion of holy ones, examples which all should
imitate, the surest guide and best comforter for
life, the strongest confirmation of our hopes in
death, and all would read and study and not
tire, and own " It is this and infinitely more."

These hints may serve to show what influence this doctrine is to have on the popular
faith. Religion is to cease to be an outward
form, the observance of the sabbath, attendance
on church, support of the clergy, the admission
of the Bible and the Saviour, the assent of the
will. It is to be a personal matter of each
man, which each must do for himself; not
mere uprightness of conduct, but positive, actual
devotion of the spirit and the heart, the strong
desire, the earnest endeavor, the hearty will to
do what is right and true ; not the negative
morality of refraining from actual sin, but the
positive virtue of acting in obedience to the dictates of Christian love ; not doing good because it is better for us, but pursuing virtue for
virtue's sake ; the religion of the spirit, not that
of the body ; in the beautiful language of one,
whose life proves that its doctrines can be carried into the daily walks of life, that religion

" whose substance is love to God, whose form is love to man, whose temple is the pure heart, whose sacrifice is a divine life."

There can be no danger from the spread of such principles ; though men may mistake the means of doing so holy a work.

MORAL OBLIGATION.

" Things right, but not expedient."

MORAL OBLIGATION.

THE character of a people is said to be determined by its religion. And the character of
its religion and its influence will be found ultimately to depend on the answer which it gives
to the question, " Why ought I to do right ? "
Let us see, then, in what the rules of duty set
forth in this system differ from others, and
whether it recognises any independent on individual inclination.

It is not proposed here to attempt to examine into the various theories which have been
advanced as the foundation of the law by which
we are bound as accountable beings. No one
could enumerate the codes of ethics which have
flourished for a time and then died, leaving to
the world nothing beside the evils attendant on
a false philosophy, but a hollow form, a worthless volume, or an empty name. All may be
resolved into these :

1. Right and justice are to be observed by man, because this will promote his happiness.

2. They are to be obeyed, because it is the law.

Now, if the low standard, which is fixed by the first rule, for human excellence, and the ruinous consequences which are its legitimate results, and to which it has always led where it has been practically adopted, were not sufficient to prove its falsity, there are other considerations which clearly show its absurdity.

It is impossible to say what happiness is, to render this rule uniform. Is it the gratification of the bodily appetites, mere animal enjoyment; or that which we derive as rational beings, the enjoyment derived from a belief that we have contributed to the common good and the approbation of men? Is it limited to this world, or does it look to the next? Things would be right or wrong, as you adopt one or the other of these definitions. Thus right and wrong would depend on man's idea of happiness.

Nor can it be shown that, by adherence to virtue, this happiness, whatever you choose to call it, will be insured. All the arguments amount only to a balance of interests, a choice of gratifications, a calculation of probabilities. But the requisite of a rule of duty is that it should be certain, known, and fixed. It is not enough to say, the gain of lying or theft is nothing compared with the evils they cause to society, and ultimately to ourselves, the pains of conscience, or the curse of evil habits; or to argue from the analogy of providence that if they are not punished in this world, they will be in another; therefore, we ought not to lie or steal. Duty must be certain, independent on interest.

If it were determined by interest, then, to know our duty, we must be able to decide what was most for our interest. Now, apart from any other rule, there is no one who could pretend to do this. The idea of duty comes before, and without any consideration of interest. At most, this would only show, could it prove all that it pretends, that if man acted prudently he would do right. If you point to his interests, he may say he will not regard them. If self alone is concerned, he may choose to follow inclination. Now this is the same as to say there is no duty, no moral obligation.

The second class differs from this only in appealing to the scriptures as an additional aid to discover what is duty. In principle it is the same. Its influence is equally debasing. Its results are equally pernicious. Paley, its great

master, states its doctrines in their most plausi-
ble form. Duty is obedience to the law of
God. This law is a prescribed rule, enforced
by rewards and punishments. In order, then,
to inquire whether we ought to do any action
or not, we are first to inquire whether we shall
be rewarded or punished for it. That is right,
which is expedient. Duty is interest. Thus,
he says, we may tell an untruth to a madman
because no evil comes of it, but rather good. It
is expedient. The true reason is, that you do
not break the moral law; you tell no lie; and
this you know whether it is expedient or not.

This, too, is a system based on the desire to
gain happiness; no higher, no better than the
other, but the same, and received only because it assumes to be based on the Scriptures. But the arguments drawn from the Bible
in its support are specious only. The righteous
will be rewarded and the wicked punished.
Admit it to be so; it does not follow that they
are righteous or wicked because they are rewarded or punished; that there is no right
without reward, no justice without expediency.
Where the Bible speaks of rewards, it is not as
conditions, but covenants. We shall have a
reward for the good, but we cannot reject it
and pay the forfeit. We are bound to it at all
events.

So we find man is appealed to as a moral being, not as a selfish one. The Scriptures are addressed to him as possessed of an instinctive and intuitive knowledge of what is right and true, and a love for it for its own sake. It is a spiritual system, not a sensual one. Right is that which the voice within approves, wrong what it condemns. Education cannot eradicate this moral sense without depriving one of an attribute of humanity. A dog may not take meat for fear of being whipped : but man is appealed to not as judging what is most for his interest, but as knowing what his duty is.

This philosophy shows the falsity of these old systems, by proving the reality of spiritual existences, what is right, true, just, beautiful, independently of interest, appetite, expediency, or association. We are to love truth because it is truth, do right because it is right. It would be strange, indeed, if man were always to act from the lowest and least worthy motives. Strange if God had implanted in the breast the highest affections without an end. Strange if God has given to man no guide in relation to his most important interests, but left him to reason out his duty under the law by arguments which must often lead to its violation. It cannot be so. There are certain things which

could not be justified to us by any arguments
of expediency. The principles of right are as
eternal as those of truth. Man knows them
from his nature, because he is man. They
need no proof.

CONCLUSION.

" Oh, joy, that in our embers
Is something that doth live ;
The spirit that remembers,
What was so fugitive."
WORDSWORTH.

CONCLUSION.

Such are some of the tendencies of Transcendentalism. It extends to man in every relation. Proposes a new rule of action wherever
he acts as man. Clearly the work to be done
is not one of a day, nor of years of ages, but of all
time. There is no danger that the world shall be
changed in a breath. It is not left to the hands of
one or a few. It is the task of the race. Each
step of humanity is one towards the goal at
which it aims. He who looks forward to see
what is to be done, who sees the evils that are
in the world which should not be there, the
false maxims and principles on which empires
are based and the human race actuated, has
need of courage and resolution of heart; but
he who will look back on the tortuous and dangerous way the child of God has thus far
travelled, and see how many that threatened his

life, born of the earth, the children of superstition and sin, have fallen dead about him, will
find enough to cheer him, and can never fear
that the race will stop or recede.

As each man is a tree, its root of sense in the
earth, its strong trunk of reason, and the holy
affections its flowers, that catch the genial
warmth of the sun, and the bland breath, and
drink in the bright light of heaven; so it is with
mankind. The ideas of the first races are all
from the earth; then from these roots of sense
springs the trunk of reason, and sooner or later
will come the fragrant blossom that mirrors
heaven, and sends new life to the roots that are
toiling for it in the earth, and the fruit that
bears the seed which secures its immortality.

The end proposed is almost too sublime for
human conception, the perfection of humanity.
The wonder is, that man should think of attaining it, with the limited means at his command,
against the obstacles he has to contend with.
It is always a task to pull down and build
anew, to renounce an old habit, though a bad
one. It gives pain to dress a wound though
that is the only remedy. A system of philosophy, on which are based our governments, our
laws, our religion, our social institutions, whose
influence extends to man every where in public

and private, if it could be demonstrated to be false as lies, would not, could not be renounced at once. All institutions, forms, doctrines, become necessary to man from use, and dear from habit and happy and holy associations. He will only see the good in these and die rather than renounce them. They are the growth of time and circumstances, and cannot be abolished at once. Though one could show every branch of our government to be bad, he must go slowly and cautiously to the work of reforming it. But the ground must be broken, the seed sown, or the harvest will be wanting. Now, this system might be engrafted on many things as they exist ; but every day adds to the difficulty. " Gold in the morning, silver in the middle of the day, lead at night." There are obstacles to its progress, for there are errors which it assails. There is danger to some institutions, for it shows their falsity. There may be danger of too much zeal, which shall rid men of the old before the new is laid hold of, but it is what every mariner runs who starts upon a voyage. There may be danger that the world is not good enough, as it is said, is not yet ready for such elevated truth. Then, in God's name, let it be made better. There are means at hand for improving the condition of

the mass of mankind, that the world little
dreams of, of relieving their wants, lightening
their burdens, cultivating their intellects, awak-
ening their religious feelings; so that the world
would wear a smile of joy at the thought of the
change that might be made in its condition.
To make most of these means is the office of
religion.   To aid this work, enforce universal
obedience, to the eternal law on which it is
founded, is the duty of man ; this task is the
end of his life.

It becomes not him, who alone is made erect,
with his face turned towards the skies, to creep
over the earth with his eyes fixed on the dust,
the image of despair.   He is the child of hope.
"Let him look to Heaven, and he will not fail
to find his home."